Signs:

What To Look For Whenever You Think You Are Being Cheated On

J. Gibson

SIGNS: WHAT TO LOOK FOR WHENEVER YOU THINK YOU ARE BEING CHEATED ON

Copyright ©2018 by J. Gibson.

Published by 7th Sign Publishing

(www.PeauxeticExpressions.com)
All rights reserved. No part of this book may be reproduced or transmitted in any form or by any means without written permission from the author/and or publisher.

Book Cover Concept by J Gibson

Book Cover Design and Illustrations by David Boyce

J. Gibson is available for keynote addresses, panel discussions, consultations, church functions, workshop events and radio/TV/internet/podcast interviews. He is also available for any book club meetings, book reviews, parties and events, anywhere in the United States. You can reach him by email at JGibsonBooks@gmail.com.

Dedication

This book is dedicated to all of the cheaters in the world. Eventually, YOU WILL be exposed.

Table Of Contents

Chapter 1:
There Is NEVER A Good Reason To Cheat — 12

Chapter 2:
Once A Cheater, Always A Cheater. Is This True? — 16

Chapter 3:
Looks Aren't Everything (They're Really Not) — 20

Chapter 4:
Emotional Cheating vs Physical Cheating — 28

Chapter 5:
Breaks and "Break Babies" — 34

Chapter 6:
Ambition and Ego — 40

Chapter 7:
Who Cheats More, Men or Women? — 46

Chapter 8:
Sex, Sex and More Sex — 54

Chapter 9:
Signs for the Fellas (What to Watch Out For) — 62

Chapter 10:
Your Words Can Control Your Relationship — 76

Chapter 11:
Signs for the Ladies (What to Watch Out For) — 82

Chapter 12:
A Little Something for the College Students — 100

Chapter 13:
The Wrap-Up   110
Bonus Chapter:
You Find Out That They Have Indeed Cheated;
Now What?   114
Extra Bonus Chapter:
"Age Ain't Nothing But A Number"…., Or So They Say 118

Something that a lot of people need to know

"When you find yourself in a relationship or marriage that you are no longer happy in, the best thing that you can do is leave that situation and walk away. To stay and to cheat or to commit infidelity is what I would call being a coward. You should never be afraid to tell your lover the TRUTH about what's happening with you and them. Because, although the TRUTH can be painful, it will set you free." – J Gibson

Introduction

Just coming off the high of writing my first book, *Men=Responsibility*, which is, by the way, a best seller. It has given me a sense of accomplishment in the literary world. Sure, I've done other things and made some wonderful strides in my life, but I have found that for me, writing is very therapeutic and relaxing.

When the idea to write this book came to me, I thought about how this would be another great read. In addition, I have some other books that I'm also presently working on writing. But, for some reason, the idea to write this particular book would not leave me alone. The title "Signs", and writing about cheating, kept coming up in my head.

The book cover design, the chapter titles, different topics, they all were in my cranium, just waiting to burst out onto paper. I have found that when a phenomenal idea comes to you, the best thing you can do is get to it right away; quickly make it a reality. Therefore, I present to you my latest literary masterpiece: *Signs: What to Look for When You Think You are Being Cheated On*.

I'll admit that I'm a former avid watcher of the TV show "Cheaters". This is probably one of the most entertaining shows that I have ever watched. From Tommy Grand, to the ever-popular Joey Greco, to the recent host and grandson of the legendary actor Clark Gable, "Cheaters" has been a staple in American society for some time now. This show has followed cheating spouses, boyfriends two-timing their girlfriends and vice versa. I have recently learned that some of the cases were staged by actors.

Yes, crazy, I know. But there is no denying that it has made for great TV in the past decade. For the cases that were real, the guilty party had no idea that private detectives were following them, observing and recording the dirt that they were involved in. Things would really begin to escalate when the host would get the person who called "Cheaters" to follow their lover and collect evidence of potential wrong doing. The party being cheated on would then get an eyewitness account of nearly everything; an up-close, personal view of the bad and the ugly.

During the interview process, the client would detail how in the beginning, everything was fine and great with their lover. But then, as time progressed, things started to change. They started noticing some "signs"; changes in their lover's behavior, indicating that there was a strong suspicion of some cheating, although initially they didn't have solid proof. Well, the good people at "Cheaters" not only got the proof, they made it possible for the client to confront their dirty-dogging lover, along with the other person, culminating in pandemonium and utter chaos.

As previously stated, it made for great television. What I want to do in this book is explain some of the "signs" you need to pay close attention to if you think, even slightly, that the person you're married to or dating, may be cheating on you. People cheat. As unfortunate as this can be, it is a reality. Enjoy the book, as we take a look at what needs to be seen, shall we?

Chapter 1
There Is NEVER A Good Reason To Cheat

You have read this correctly! No one will ever be able to explain to you that cheating is a good thing, nor can they tell anyone that cheating is justifiable. They just can't. No matter how bad a marriage or relationship is going, to mess around and cheat on your lover is wrong. This is absolutely not the way to go. When one cheats, they are committing a serious act of betrayal. Here's why:

You're in a relationship and things start to go south. You and your significant other are having problems…, you're wondering if those problems can be fixed. Then, one person in the relationship starts seeing someone else. Guess what? You can believe that the person that's stepping out on their lover is doing so in a totally secretive way. They may be somewhat unhappy in their current situation, but for some reason, they don't want to end their present relationship and simply move on.

No…the cheater opts to keep who they are presently in a relationship with, while simultaneously fooling around with some new "meat". They start lying about where they are, where they're going, and who they're seeing and spending time with. That's called "betrayal", plain and simple. And here's the kicker: the person doing the dirty deed has to know that if they were found out to be cheating, they would lose their longtime relationship and quite possibly the new thing, if both people found out.

What plausible reason could this person who cheated have given for cheating in the first place? That's just it, people...there is no viable reason to be given. If your relationship is going sour, and if you and that person have attempted to fix your relationship with, seemingly no resolution, you should break up and move on, bottom line. What you shouldn't do is start something new with someone else, while you're still in a current marriage/relationship. That's wrong...all it does is create chaos, even if the chaos is subtle.

I know it sounds like I'm preaching here, and if that's the case, then so be it. Someone needs to tell it like it is. There is never an excuse for someone to cheat on their lover. As you read this book, you'll see some logical, intricate reasons as to why it is never a good thing to cheat on anyone.

You'll also see how you can notice some signs of possible deceit if you suspect that the one you love is two-timing you. Turn the page and keep reading.

Chapter 2
Once A Cheater, Always A Cheater. Is This True?

Now, this has been a raging debate for many years, with people on both sides of the spectrum having their say. Some would say that people who have cheated in the past can change and not do it again, while you have those who completely believe that if someone cheats one time, they are bound to do it again and again.

One of the best indicators of this is to point out a person's past behavior. For example, if you have a person who has been in relationships and they have been guilty of cheating on their lovers, almost one after the other, most likely they will continue to display that type of behavior, without fail. Some of this can be attributed to that person or those people being betrayed by others, and not letting go of those hurts. Some of them have the mindset of "well, I was misled, so why don't I do the same thing that was done to me". You see, this is a classic example of "hurt people, hurting other people".

Those people that were hurt by someone else will turn around and dish out what was done to them.

This cycle of bad behavior has been going on for eons now. It's crazy. Now, why do I call it bad behavior? Well, think about it; you're in a relationship with someone and you believe that everything is fine. But then you find out that the one you're with is cheating on you. You find out that they have been lying and deceiving you, and you're crushed by their betrayal.

Now ask yourself, is this bad behavior or what? Hell yes, it's bad behavior. I don't personally know anyone who would think that this is a great way to act. And I'll speak for myself, from a hypothetical stance. If I were to suffer a setback and my girl cheated on me with another man, and I forgave her and we stayed together, do I think that she would cheat again? I wouldn't come out and say "Yeah, she would.", but I'd be lying if I said it wouldn't be in the back of my mind.

If someone who cheats on their lover doesn't feel the slightest bit of remorse about what they have done, chances are they are going to do it again. Hypothetically, if I were cheated on, I can't say that it wouldn't happen again by the same person. Now, in order for a person to become rehabilitated from not being a cheater and wanting to shed the "once a cheater always a cheater" moniker, they have to first recognize that they were wrong for what they have done and acknowledge it. Unless a person does this, they can't get on the road to turning their life around and changing their ways.

Anyone can change, but they have to want to change, bottom line. Take, for example, the unfaithful person who does cheat. Did you know that some people who cheat will sometimes blame the person that they are in a relationship with or married to for cheating? Yes, some who are guilty of being philanderers tend to put the blame for what they did on their longtime lover. They will say they did it because they weren't getting enough sex, enough support, or something else in some capacity.

Certain studies have shown that a person who behaves in this manner will more than likely continue this pattern of behavior throughout all of their relationships. These people are what I would call "pass the buck" people. "Pass the buck" people are individuals, who never accept any responsibility for their actions, and rather than cop to the decisions that they chose to make, they choose to not accept responsibility; they "pass the buck" to others.

Understand that people who live their lives like this will have no sympathy or feelings of remorse with regard to how they treat others. This is a shame. Now, like I said earlier, cheaters can change their ways, but not only do they have to want to change, the person who was cheated on has to be open-minded and receptive to it. The cheater has to work hard to regain the trust of the person that they betrayed.

Sometimes, that's easy, and sometimes, it's not easy. But with hard work, lots of open communication from both people and most importantly, quality time spent together, anything is possible. Is it true that once a cheater, always a cheater? I'll let you, the reader, decide on that.

Chapter 3
Looks Aren't Everything
(They're Really Not)

This is going to be a deep chapter, so buckle up! When it comes to men and women, and the business of cheating, physical attraction tends to be an important thing. When it comes to men, we look at everything on a woman. We see titties, the curve of her butt, her legs, face, hair…, everything. With women, it's a little different. They see broad shoulders, his height, how he wears his clothes, his face, his hair, and so forth.

Similar to how we approach food, we eat with our eyes. If a certain dish on the menu looks good to us, we tend to gravitate towards ordering that dish. The same can be said about how men look at women. If she "looks" good to our eyes, that is what we will go after. I'm a man, so I can attest to this. When a man chooses to cheat on his main lady with another woman, you can believe most of his decision rested on how that other woman looked. Because, for the most part, men are visual; they go after what looks good.

In some cases, a man that cheats on his wife/girlfriend doesn't have to necessarily do it because he's having problems in his present relationship. He just wanted to see what this other fine woman was working with, just for kicks. In other words, he cheated because the other woman looked too good to pass up, even if his wife/girlfriend looked equally good, if not better. Isn't that amazing? This is what a lot of men have been doing for a long time, cheating on their women, seemingly just for the hell of it.

As for women, they can and have been cheating with men who look somewhat better than their husbands/boyfriends. Yes, women are visual as well, but most of the time, when they cheat on the husband/boyfriend, they will cheat with a reason behind it. One reason could be to get back at their lover for cheating on them, and they will look for the man who looks like a younger Denzel Washington. And don't let him look like that actor Christian Keyes! Oh man, some will drool and pull down their panties in a heartbeat. Not all women get down like this, but a lot of them do.

Now, what I want to discuss in this chapter is why it's important for both men and women to know this: <u>everyone who looks good to you is not good</u>

for you. I'll give a great example from the man's standpoint. Do you remember Tyler Perry's stage play, *Why Did I Get Married*? If not, here's a brief rundown. It was demonstrated in the characters of Mike and Sheila.

Mike and Sheila were married for years. Mike started straying from his wife because she was starting to gain weight. Sheila had a good friend name Trina. Trina was slim and fine, something that most men gravitate towards. Consequently, Mike decides to have an affair with Trina. Mind you, Sheila seems like a wonderful wife to Mike, but because she was a bit bigger than Mike's liking, he decides to take up with her best friend. Sheila finds out and is devastated, of course.

Fast forward into the story. Mike finds out that Trina is lazy and a gold digger. Sheila, on the other hand, bounces back from the betrayal, loses some weight and takes up with Troy, who is there for Sheila during her heartbreak from Mike and Trina. After some time to reflect on his life choices, Mike later realized that he had made a grave mistake and he began to miss Sheila, who has now moved on from Mike and is happy with the other guy.

At this point, you may wonder why I have included this common scenario? Well, it's simple. What Mike thought he wanted in a woman, he already had that and then some in Sheila. But, because she gained some weight and wasn't looking her best in his eyes, he started looking elsewhere for companionship. He found it in another pretty and attractive woman, but it wasn't what he thought it would be. Mike had a real treasure in Sheila, but he chased after trash in Trina, resulting in his ultimate regret for a major mistake and a bad decision.

There are plenty of men who do the same thing. They chase after what looks good to the naked eye, without thinking about the unseen intangibles. What are some unseen intangibles that I'm referring to? Well, for starters, one of them could be how a woman handles money. Is she a spendthrift or a saver? Another one could be this: is she all about herself; does she do things that will only please her, or is she selfless and looking to do for others?

What I'm saying here is just because a woman looks good doesn't mean that she's a good person. The same thing could be said for women about men. Most of them want the guy with six pack abs, muscles everywhere on his body; tall, dark and handsome. But what they may not realize is that most of these types of men may be self-absorbed people who only look to take from a woman, without having a desire to give to a woman. Some women will pass over the so-called "dorky, funny looking man" and will go for the good-looking, muscle-built man with 'good' hair.

Also, I'll add this too. Some of these good-looking men have NO problem slapping a woman, hitting a woman or beating the holy hell out of a woman. What I am driving at for both men and women is this: you cannot tell what type a person someone is just by looking at them. You have to give yourself time to get to know them and to see what type of character that person has. Only focusing on the physical make up of a person won't give you that much needed insight as to who they are as a person.

This statement that I'm about to make is a true one that will do you good to live by: "W*hen you fall in love with a person's soul, that one person will be all you need and desire; but when you chase after the superficial things like how someone looks to the naked eye, no one will ever* *satisfy you, because you will always be searching for perfection, which you'll never find"*.

While I won't discount the fact that people do make mistakes and commit acts of treachery that they shouldn't, please understand that we shouldn't want to mess up a happy home by thinking that when we see someone who may look better than the person that we are currently with, we should go after them. They may be attractive, fun and outgoing, and they may give us something that we think we're missing at home, but you could be making a big mistake that you can't come back from.

Always appreciate what you have and if you think that your lover is not looking their best, be active and tactful in getting them to where you would like to see them. That means to the men reading this book, give your wife/girlfriend a much-needed makeover, help her lose some weight, or help buy her a new wardrobe. If you have a car that needs repairing in some way, are you going to go out and buy another car? No, you're going to do what you can to fix your current vehicle and keep it moving. Well, give your woman that same consideration.

Do what you can to fix what you already have, instead of going out and searching for a "better looking" woman. You may have a rare gem in your possession already, and instead of polishing that gem up, you go out and look for rhinestones. Gems have far more value than some cheap rhinestone; they always will have more value.

For the ladies reading this book, if you want your husband/boyfriend to look good for you, encourage him tactfully to go to the gym, and eat better. Whether you believe it or not, we men love for our ladies to give us words of encouragement. That will motivate us to want to be the man you want and desire.

If he treats you good and takes care of what he's supposed to as a man, stay with that man and build him up, instead of going out and searching to be with a good-looking piece of garbage. Let's be honest, some 'good-looking' as well as some 'not-so-good-looking' men are garbage. Remember, appreciate what you have in who you are with. Please know that looks aren't everything. All that glitters is not gold.

Chapter 4
Emotional Cheating vs Physical Cheating

Now in this chapter, I will talk about how this is a gray area for so many people. Which is worse in your opinion, being an emotional cheater or cheating in the physical sense? Personally, I would say that they're somewhat equally bad, but there are those that would disagree with me, and that's fine.

As best as I can, I'll explain the difference between the two. Of course, physical cheating is bad and horrible. This is where one finds themselves spending time with, doing things with and having sexual relations with someone other than their significant other whom they've been with for a long period of time, and are still currently with.

Physical cheating entails someone who is living a double life, only existing to fulfill their own selfish desires. Emotional cheating is a little different. This is where one finds themselves thinking about and fantasizing about someone other than who they're currently with, and in some cases wishing they were with that person.

When you're in a marriage or relationship, you have to be "all in". What I mean by that is you have to be willing to give who you're with all of you, all of the time. You have to give that person your mind, body and soul, because you have chosen to connect with that person on a deep and spiritual level. When someone is cheating, they are spreading themselves between who they're with in a current marriage/relationship, and the person they're being sneaky and conniving with, simultaneously.

Even if you're not cheating physically, but you still find yourself detached emotionally from your lover, you are in a bad spot. In other words, you can be there with your husband or wife, or your boyfriend or girlfriend in the physical sense, but not mentally or emotionally. Like I said before, you have to be all in with your marriage or relationship. Otherwise, or what's the point of being with that person?

Think about this as well. If someone sees that they're emotionally cheating on their lover, eventually they may just step it up and cheat in the physical sense. Why? It's because those feelings to be with that other person won't go away all on their own. That person who is emotionally detached will have to kill those feelings of wanting to be with someone other than the person they're married to or in a long-term relationship with.

This is one of the biggest reasons why relationships take so much work; but more importantly, why people have to be comfortable in the choice they made to be married or in a relationship. As time progresses, a marriage or relationship can get stale, boring, lifeless and unfulfilling without the proper work and care.

The temptation to be with someone new is present for people all the time, and if someone decides not to cheat in the physical sense, they can still secretly desire to be with someone else, emotionally. Someone who looks better than their lover, someone who seems more interesting than their lover, or someone who can seemingly offer more to them then their current lover can.

Whether it's cheating physically or emotionally, it's still cheating at the end of the day. You are not giving your all to the person you're with, and that can spell the end of your marriage/relationship, if and only if you don't check it and correct it.

Imagine making love to your lover, you're in the groove, and on the surface everything appears to be just fine. But, while you're physically sexing up your lover, mentally and emotionally, you're with someone else; someone that you have been secretly desiring. Don't you think that at some point, you may want to explore being with that person physically, as opposed to just desiring the other person emotionally?

As previously stated, if you don't check it and correct it, you'll end up following through on your physical desires, and quite possibly messing up a good thing with your current lover in the process. You will wake up thinking about that other person, go through your day thinking about that other person, even while simply eating a meal or just lounging, you will find yourself thinking about that other person. Either way, you can't have a successful marriage/relationship if you find yourself being a cheater, physically or emotionally. This is the bottom line.

In addition, most of the time that a man leaves a woman to be with another woman, he has left physically first, then he leaves emotionally. In contrast, when a woman leaves a man for another man, she leaves emotionally first and then physically. This is an important thing to understand about cheating.

Chapter 5
Breaks and "Break Babies"

I was listening to a radio show recently, and a young lady called in and told the host that she recently had to break up with her boyfriend of 5 years, all because he needed a "break". Yes, this dude told her that he felt like they were moving too fast, after being together for 5 years, mind you, he needed a "break" from the relationship.

I can only imagine how she initially felt after hearing those words come out of his mouth. Now, if you are reading this book and you are smart, as I know you are, ask yourself this: "Why do you think that this dude wanted to take a break from his girl?" Let me take a stab at answering this one. It's more than likely because he wanted to step away from her, in order to get acquainted to some "new meat". And, after getting up close to that "new meat" and having his way with it, he wanted the option of getting back with his woman.

There is this seemingly new thing where couples don't break up with each other for good. What they seem to be doing is taking "breaks" from each other, and testing the waters with other people, only to get back together with their longtime lover later down the road. Now, I must say that this is some immature 'poppycock'. No one should tolerate this from anyone.

If you're with someone, and you both are flowing and growing together, why do you feel the need to take a break? What is that all about? You either should be all in and staying with each other or you break up for good and move on to someone else. There should be no gray area where you can 'hold your place in line' and come back if you don't like what else is out there.

"Break Babies". Yes, this is something crazy that people are now engaging in. This is where someone takes a break from whomever they are with, goes off and produces a baby with another person, then ultimately gets back with their previous lover. Now, you are back together with your ex, but you now have made a baby with someone else. Consequently, life has become extra complicated for you.

At this juncture, I am going to boldly give examples, by naming some famous people: people that most of us are familiar with. The rapper, Ludacris, created a "break baby" with another woman, only to marry his longtime girlfriend, after that baby was created. Another one is basketball superstar Dwayne Wade, who is married to actress Gabrielle Union. From what I understand, the baby that Dwayne made with the other woman can't come anywhere near Gabrielle Union. Does this make sense to anyone?

Two men, who for whatever reason took a break from their women, got with other women, had unprotected sex and got the other women pregnant, only to get back with the ladies they took a break from. (On a personal note…, I can't imagine why those guys wouldn't wear a condom when they had sex with the other women…, but I digress.) Men are going to do what they want.

I mentioned these two guys who have celebrity status, who went off and did this, but understand that they are far from the only men in the world who have made "break babies" with other women, only to get back with the women that they were with in the beginning.

The reason I have included this chapter in this book is to expose some acts of serious, emotionally and possibly physically damaging games that people tend to engage in.

Now, I'll speak to the ladies for a brief moment. If you have been with a man for some time, and you believe that everything is fine between the two of you, but one day he tells you that he needs to take a "break" from you, this is a huge sign that things are not fine with you and him.

You can be fairly certain that if he takes that desired "break" from you, he's going to go to another woman or several other women. Honestly, after which time, you'd be a fool to take him back. What you would be doing is in affect giving him carte blanche to go off and do what he wants, only to come running back to you when he's done playing around. Ask yourself this: 'How do you think things would be for you and him if he were to go and make a baby with another woman?' You can rest assured that things will be hectic. Only you can answer if you would want that stress in your life.

Now, I'll speak to the fellas. Real talk. It's gotten hard out here for women to find a good man. When they feel like they have found one, the last thing they want to do is take a 'break'. They are with you, dating you to see if you are potential husband material. If you can't decide whether that woman is the one for you, you probably don't want to play games with her; taking "breaks" because you're confused.

I would advise you to be honest, truthful and forthcoming with that woman. Either stay with her and build a future, or decide that she's not the one for you, let her go and allow her to find her "Mr. Right". But, what you shouldn't do is play games, take breaks, and go screw around with other women, only to come running back to her, because you are selfish and don't want her to be truly happy.

If you do that while you and she are not married, what's to stop you from doing this after you exchange vows? I would venture to say "nothing".

Like I said before, I'm not pulling any punches in this book. I'm only interested in giving all of my readers of this book the real deal. I personally don't believe that people should take "breaks" from each other. All this does is provide time for someone to do whatever they want, only to have the option to come back to familiarity. If this type of activity continues to happen in our society, most people won't really have true happiness in their lives.

Honestly, I'm tired of seeing women, particularly black women, alone and pissed off about some no-good man who decided he needed a "break". This last line is how I personally feel, but hopefully you understand where I'm coming from overall. Taking a "break" from your boyfriend/girlfriend can only spell trouble, especially if you plan on coming back to them. Think about everything that I've said here, and pay attention to people's motives. Life is too short for the drama and bull crap.

Chapter 6
Ambition and Ego

Now, I have to include this chapter, because this is an issue that can be subtle but damaging for most relationships. There are couples in which the man and the woman are both high achievers. They work hard and smart for what they have acquired in their lives. On the flip side, there are couples where one person may be a little more successful than the other person; depending on the level of understanding or lack thereof in that relationship, this could pose a problem for those couples.

I'll give an example of what I mean. There is a movie that I recently high-jacked from the library, based on different married couples and a case of infidelity. One couple in particular is having problems wherein the wife doesn't want to be a housewife anymore, therefore, she goes back to work, because she's bored at home and she wishes to utilize her college degree.

On turn, the husband has a huge problem with this, because he feels that her working outside of the home, is taking away from her being there for him and the kids. In one scene, she is preparing to attend a function where she is being honored with an award, and the husband is going to their daughter's dance recital. They have a big argument, and he ends up telling her that he doesn't support the fact that she has a career.

Fast forward near the end of the movie, and he reveals to her that he's had an affair and the other woman is pregnant. The wife is livid and she kicks the husband out of the home they share.

Now, the reason I added this part into this chapter is to show you, the reader, that the husband cheated on his wife, not because she was doing something wrong, but because it would appear that his ego was affected by his wife's ambition to do something more than to just be a simple housewife.

This is where I talk about ambition and ego. This can be a problem in most relationships. When a couple is together and growing, there should be harmony from the standpoint that when one person in the relationship is attempting to achieve something great and wonderful, their significant other should be their biggest cheerleader: the person with whom they share the highs and lows of their undertaking.

Amazingly, what I have found in doing some research for this chapter is that some men don't necessarily want the women in their lives to rise to a certain point, either economically or socially. That's crazy, right? It's crazy, yet it holds so true. Not all men get down like this, but there are factions of men in the world who don't want an overachieving wife/girlfriend in their lives, because it makes them feel small.

Yes, there are men who feel that a woman doing something big that pays them well and gives them both recognition will give him an inferiority complex. To put it plainly, some men can't handle a woman of substance or worth. It's hard to fully explain why there are men who are like this. Men that possess this negative characteristic are an abomination to the overall success of the couple, as a whole.

Here's a significant point… most women want to be with a man who works hard and has ambition to do better in his life. When a woman comes across a man like this, she will be his biggest, and in some cases, his only supporter. So why can't some men reciprocate that same support to their women? Here is the answer in one word; insecurity.

Some men are so insecure, to the point where they feel that if a woman is doing well, and they're not matching her ambition, she might take off and leave him.

Fellas, I have to tell you that you have to have enough confidence and be secure enough within yourself that you are a sufficient mate, just as you are, without clinging to the negative inclination that you will be 'replaced' if your woman is climbing the corporate ladder or making great strides in the business world. If you love her, and she loves you and you both support each other, then cheer her on when she achieves something that she's been working towards. People have to understand that a huge ingredient of a successful relationship is being fully supportive of the person you're married to or dating.

Now, allow me to mention this to the ladies.... Some of you have a bad habit of rubbing your successes in a man's face, making it seem like he's not a real man because he's not making the type of money you're making. This is an unattractive and obstructive trait! That is one of the quickest ways to poison your relationship with that man.

Most of us men understand that we are living in a time where women are making huge strides in the business world, having the title of CEO and other great things that women are now doing. However, what you don't want to do is make the man in your life feel small by flaunting your successes in his face, in a negative way. Some women do this, but, this is a negative attribute that you must refrain from. Please know that it is possible to be successful and humble at the same time.

There are plenty of successful single women out here. This is due in part to some of these women feeling like a man has to be on her level: if he's not, then he's not the man for her. Arrogance in a woman is a huge turn off to the fellas, ladies. Listen; there is nothing wrong with a man or woman having ambition for themselves.

You only have one shot at this thing called "life" and you should want to live it to the fullest. However, no one should ever be intimidated or insecure because of another person's success. A man should not allow his ego to be bruised because his woman wants to be more that his arm candy. In turn, a woman should not rub the fact that she's a multi-million-dollar business woman in her man's face, thinking that he should be doing the same thing.

A couple should support one another in whatever dreams and desires they may have, and cheer lead each other's accomplishments, always. If a couple doesn't do that, they are opening the door for cheating and infidelity to enter in. All of that can be avoided. Love and support the one you're with: keep your union intact.

Chapter 7
Who Cheats More, Men or Women?

This chapter promises to be intriguing. A recent study done with *Women's Health Magazine* showed that out of almost 1000 men and women surveyed to find out who cheats more, nearly half of the women said that they have strayed at some point in a relationship. Even though the numbers still favor men cheating more than the women, it is not by a large margin. I found this interesting, considering that men seem to cheat left and right, and have been doing so for centuries.

Now, here is my thought on the matter...you're more than welcome to disagree with me. I personally tend to believe that men, yes, us men, tend to cheat much more than the ladies. I'll explain what I mean.

For the most part, most men don't really need much of a reason to cheat. All most of us need is an opportunity and a willing accomplice... BAM! It's a done deal. Cheating for some men almost comes naturally.

What I have found is that most men who are with a woman who is their wife/girlfriend are happy and to a degree; basically satisfied with their partner. But, as time progresses with their partner, they tend to get bored. Bored how? Well, they may get bored with being with the same woman, day in and day out. The same booty, the same thong panties, the same pair of breast, the same hairy or bald vagina, the same face and/or the same skin tone. Now don't misunderstand, if they're getting sex on the regular from that woman, they don't see anything wrong with that. It's just that some men like variety from time to time.

I've even heard one guy say that he doesn't want to eat "skittles" all the time when talking about being monogamous with his lady. He said that he may want skittles one day, then he may want a Snicker's candy bar another day, and then he may want Laffy Taffy on the weekend. You get this? This guy has compared being with women to eating candy. Crazy, I know. But, this is the reality of some men in the world. Basically lacking care and respect for his wife/girlfriend's feelings, he is only interested in his own selfish desires.

As this relates to women, it's a little different. Yes, women do cheat too, and some of them cheat almost as frequently as men. But when women cheat, it's most often for a deeper reason than why men cheat. There are some women who cheat as a way to get back at a man who's cheated on her first. This is what's known as "revenge cheating". When someone engages in this behavior, they don't necessarily want to break up or get a divorce from their lover; they just want that person to know what it feels like to be cheated on.

Some women tend to act out as payback in this manner. And, as for the guy that the women will cheat with, more than likely, he will be someone that she knows. An old friend that she's known for some years; or, in some cases, she may even cheat with someone her lover knows, just to really stick it to her lover for doing her dirty. In other words, she didn't just cheat to be cheating like most men tend to do. There was a motive behind her act. Thus, there is a difference in the reason why men cheat and why women cheat.

Now, let's rewind a bit. I mentioned earlier as to how some men tend to want variety in their lives when it comes to the ladies. I have to interject some degree of equality in this stance. There are some women who want to also seek variety as well, desiring to "mix it up" with regard to the men they deal with. But, do know that their desire for variety isn't all based on looks, like men tend to primarily seek.

For example, there are some women who will want to be exclusive with one man, but he may not be able to provide her with everything she wants and needs. Most women want a man who can throw down in the bedroom, but what if his money is not long enough for her? What she will do is get a second man; one who has long money, but that man may not be handsome enough for her. Thus, in turn, she will then get with a third man; one who turns heads when he walks down the street because he's so good looking, but his "stroke game" is weak.

Has the picture been vividly painted for you, in this example? I have given you a scenario in which three men, all provide something for different for this one woman, all while she may be in a committed relationship with someone who makes her happy, but not happy enough for her to want to be monogamous.

She's cheating on her lover with several other men: each one that does some distinct thing for her, at any given time. One guy is good-looking;

arm candy for her; the other guy gives her great sex, and yet an additional guy doesn't mind spending his money on her. In essence, she's cheating on her main lover, and she thinks that this is totally fine.

You see, men may cheat a bit more than women, but you have some women out here that are just as bad. Moreover, I have to add this in order to make my point crystal clear: I truly believe that men tend to be sloppy cheaters, while women tend to be the cunning cheaters: the ones that cheat with stealth and thought to their movements.

Let me break down the difference here... When a man is getting some extra 'loving' on the side, from someone other than his wife/girlfriend, he will sometimes let it go to his head (the head on his shoulders), and allow it to inflate his ego. In doing so, he tends to mess up and get sloppy with his indiscretions, without really thinking about his actions.

For example, he'll leave a burner phone that he calls his "side women" on lying somewhere that his main girl is bound to find it. Or, he may tend to text those other women from his main phone, not realizing that his main lady likes playing "Candy Crush" on his phone, and she ultimately finds the texts between him and other women.

Here's another good example:
If he and his main lady do not use condoms when they have sex, and he uses condoms with his other women, he may slip up and leave those condoms inside of his vehicle, forgetting to take them out. He and his main lady hops into his "ride" one night to go somewhere, she finds the condoms, a huge argument ensues, resulting in him trying to come up with some wild lie as to why she found condoms in his ride and they don't even use them. Yep. This is the sloppy behavior that some men have that I'm talking about.

Women, on the other hand, tend to be subtle with their sneaky dealings. They will meet a man at their friend's home, the friend who is sworn to secrecy, vowing not to tell anything. And chances are, they will not allow egos to cause them to slip up and get caught. They will use creative ways to contact the other man or men, without using their main cell phone to do so.

Now, please keep in mind that no one is perfect. The aforementioned scenarios do not apply to all women who cheat, just the smarts ones who may have been caught in the past and have learned their lessons.

Hey fellas, I'm not trying to throw you under the bus when I say that most of you are sloppy cheaters; I'm just stating facts. Lots of men have been busted cheating by their main lady, due to some minor mistake that they failed to not make. One thing that no one can ever accuse me of is giving cheating a pass.

The primary goal in this book is to 'chop up' game by describing how people have been behaving for a long time. People cheat on each other, which is an unfortunate reality. They shouldn't, but they do.

As you, the reader, continue to read this book, I'll show you what I believe to be some signs that you, man or woman, should look for if you think that your lover is cheating and doing you dirty.

Chapter 8
Sex, Sex and More Sex...

I surmise that I will have some fun explaining this chapter, seeing as how when it comes to people and cheating, sex is pretty much at the root of it all. First, I'll approach opening this chapter from the standpoint of why I believe men cheat more than women. Sex! Men love sex, men need sex, men crave sex, and men are always thinking about sex.

Remember the movie *Baby Boy*? There is a scene where Jody and Yvette are having a heated conversation after she finds condoms in her car, knowing full well that she and Jody didn't use condoms whenever they had intercourse. After prodding Jody for some answers, he finally broke down and told Yvette what she didn't want to hear. He said to her "I make love to you, but I screw other females from time to time. I don't know why I do it, I just do".

This is the case with a lot of men out here. They can have a wife/girlfriend at home who gives them sex on the regular, but sometimes, even that won't be enough to quench a man's desire to have sex with other women. Some of this can be attributed to how men view women. Some men don't view women as human beings with feelings and emotions. Some men view women as sexual objects, with pretty faces to be licked and kissed on, with big breasts to be sucked on and squeezed, with big juicy booties to be smacked on and grabbed, and with vaginas to be licked, sucked and penetrated.

I'm not pulling any punches here, as you can see. The man with the wife/girlfriend at home has all of this in his reach, but for many men, her breast, booty, vagina, and face are not enough for him. So, he cheats with other women, all to fulfill his need for sexual intercourse with different women.

What are some of the motives as to why he may desire sex with other women? Here are some reasons that could be the case: His main lady may not like having oral sex, so he will find a woman or women who loves to "slob the knob", in so many words. Or, he may be into anal sex, and his main lady says "hell no" to that. So, instead of being fine with not being able to insert his penis into that tighter, more taboo 'orifice' of hers, he will find a woman who is totally fine with him entering her "back door", if you catch my meaning.

Here's the thing. If a man wants to be faithful to his partner, then he is going to have to be fine with the way they have sex. If she's not into anal sex, oral sex, swinging, threesomes or really rough sex, he needs to be fine with that. Otherwise, he should not be married or in a long-term relationship. That's just my own personal belief.

Now, on to the ladies... Women love sex too! Yes, they do. They may all not like it to the extent that a man likes it, but they love it as well. For women, I don't believe that they are as intricate as men can be when it comes to body parts, although most of them do want a man that can come with that thunder in the bedroom and make them climb the walls.

And, for the record, in case you were wondering about this, ladies: SIZE DOES MATTER. But here's the swerve: a man's penis size can be a good thing and a bad thing. What do I mean? Well, there are women who like men that are hung like thoroughbred horses. Likewise, there are women who don't necessarily like that in a man. The ones that do like a man with a big "Johnson" may think that his "stroke game" is off the chain. This can be true in some cases, while not so true in others.

Here's the reality. Just because a man is packing some big meat, it doesn't necessarily mean that he knows how to work it good in the bedroom. On the flip side of this, I have heard some women say that they don't necessarily like a well-endowed man, because he can hurt their vaginal walls with that 'big monster' of his... resulting in uncomfortable sex, even though he's working with a lot between his legs. Nonetheless, the men that are packing and can stroke like a champ, are the men that most women desire!

In turn, some women are fine with a man who has an average size penis, for the record. When it comes down to what some women want and why they cheat, it is this: some husbands/boyfriends may not like performing oral sex on a woman, because they think it's nasty. So, some women will go out and find a man who loves giving fellatio, without reservation. She, therefore will cheat on her man with a habitual "coochie-eater".

Some women want a man who's into "golden showers". If her husband/boyfriend is not the type of dude who wants his woman peeing on him during sex, she may be inclined to go out and find a man who is into that activity, as crazy as it sounds. What I'm ultimately getting at in this chapter is people tend to have weird sexual desires and fetishes: they eventually want to be able to express those desires with their lover. But, if they find that a certain fetish or fetishes is too much for their lover, and the lover won't budge to please them, they may cheat. Is it right? No, but it is some people's reality.

Something else I'll add herein... There are some couples that are dealing with the fact that the man is a premature ejaculator; meaning that every time he has sex with his wife/girlfriend, he tends to "blow his load" early, and his lady is left sexually unfulfilled. This can be a real problem for couples.

If the problem is not fixed, the sexually frustrated woman may be inclined to go out and cheat on her husband/boyfriend with a man who can stroke and stroke and stroke, allowing the woman to have multiple orgasms and then some. The woman who cheated may feel justified in doing so, because as much as she loves her lover, his incapacity to last long during sex was too much for her to take. Although this is still not justifiable reason to cheat, her anguish is somewhat understandable.

Here is a remedy that couples can experiment with to overcome premature ejaculation. Ladies, before you and your lover have sex, give your man a hand job and make him cum, allowing that first load to be gotten out of the way. Then, you wait. Go have dinner, go catch a movie, go do some laundry, go and read a book or go catch up on your favorite TV show.

Later, when your lover can get another erection, he should be ready to have sex with you and he should last longer. By him getting that first load out of his system, only to get another erection a few hours later, he should last longer because he's had an earlier ejaculation already. It should take him a while to get a second one in the same day.

Now, while I'm no sex expert, this is a trick that a sex therapist stated on TV one time that tends to help couples where the man tends to "bust a nut" faster during sex than he needs to. Again, there are other things that a couple can discuss regarding the areas by which their sex life is hurting and in need of repair. But, they should be comfortable discussing these things and having open and constant communication with each other.

When you think about when it comes to sex, one of the reasons why cheating happens so often is because the couple who is having issues won't talk to each other, out of fear of being rejected, or embarrassment. No couple should ever be afraid to communicate with each other, because communication is the life blood of a successful relationship. In other words, people have to be willing to talk to each other.

How is Johnny supposed to know that Jennifer doesn't like her vagina being sucked on and licked on, and Johnny enjoys giving oral sex to a female? Or, how is Sonya supposed to know that Michael likes having his penis sucked, and Sonya is repulsed by the thought of performing that sexual act?

In order for there to be harmony and an understanding of what is desired and not desired in the bedroom, couples have to talk and communicate with each other. If they don't get a verbal understanding, someone is bound to cheat, seeking what they want from someone else. This happens all the time with couples: someone cheated because the communication was severely lacking.

I'm speaking truth to empower people, so pay attention! Overall, my aim in this chapter is to get you, the reader, to understand that it's possible for a committed couple to have a successful relationship and a viable sex life without having to cheat with someone else in order to be fulfilled. An understanding of what both people want and expect is needed before you move forward in wanting to be with one another.

If you're with someone and they have desires/fetishes that you may not be up to fulfilling, get that understood right away. Don't allow a lack of understanding to cause you to cheat, or be cheated on. When you know better, you tend to do better; which makes you are a better person in the long run.

Chapter 9
Signs for the Fellas
(What to Watch Out For)

Now, this is where I get into the meat of this book... No one wants to be cheated on, ever. But it does happen and sometimes the signs of the other person doing their dirt can be squarely in your face, without you even knowing it. What I want to do is share some signs that you can look for and pay attention to, if you think that your wife/girlfriend is stepping out on you and seeing another man.

Now, before I start with this I just want to say that if you ever think that there is some funny business going on with your girl, keep your eyes open and have some concrete proof. If you don't do that, and you accuse her of cheating, she may try to turn it around and say that you're doing the very thing you're accusing her of doing.

Have your ducks in a row before you start making accusations. Now, here are some signs to pay attention to if you suspect cheating on the part of your wife/girlfriend:

1. Women tend to use the bathroom quite often during the course of a day. If she is always taking her phone with her while she relieves herself, she may be cheating. Before you accuse her of anything though, may certain you have some proof. You don't want to accuse her without any proof. This could do some damage to your union.

2. The only time a sexy woman with a nice frame wears "granny" panties is for that "time of the month" week. If she is always wearing "granny" panties with you, but she puts on thong panties when she goes somewhere without you, she may be cheating.

3. If she always nags you about taking her out and having fun and if you don't change your ways, then after a while, she may stop asking you to take her out altogether. You may suggest going out and having some fun, but she turns you down. Pay attention to her fellas, because she may have already

started going out with someone else, without you even knowing it.

4. If you have cheated a few times in the past on the same woman, and she has not left you yet, look out! Almost assuredly she will cheat as payback. This is only a speculation though, so don't go thinking that she's plotting to cheat on you. Just stay alert.

5. If you and she were once social media friends, but something happened where she "unfriended" you on Facebook or unfollowed you on Twitter/Instagram, she may be cheating on you.

6. Here's a good one: Let's say you're the type of person whose career takes you out of town quite often, and you ask your "homeboy" to look after your girl. If you begin to notice that after time she and he start to get somewhat close, there is probably something going on with them. Pay attention, because many guys have

been betrayed by their so-called close "homeboy".

7. Here is another interesting one: If you or your lady are military, you both may want to solidify an understanding with each other. Those long overseas deployments can wreak havoc in a marriage/relationship. Couples have broken up due to infidelity because one person needed some sexual healing, and their spouse or lover was thousands of miles away. If you know that you're the type of person that can't stand a long-distance relationship, you don't need to be involved with a person that's in the military, or if you are the military person yourself. Be honest with yourself on this one. Successful relationships rarely happen when the people don't see one another on a regular basis.

8. If she is the type of person who loves going to strip clubs with her girls, pay attention to this. Those male strippers with their

muscular bodies have a way of mesmerizing women out of their panties. If her visits become almost disturbingly frequent, she may be cheating on you with a male exotic dancer.

9. If you and she share a bank account and you start noticing money coming up missing... you know you haven't touched the money... you confront her about the missing money and she can't explain it, she may be spending that money on another man.

10. If you have started gaining weight and not looking as buff as you use to look... she not only starts complaining about how you look, she also starts comparing you to other buff men..., if this goes on for some time, she may be cheating.

11. If she is always complimenting dudes on social media, and "liking" their photos and other things: you complain about how this

makes you uncomfortable, but she does it anyway, despite being told that you don't like it, she could be cheating.

12. If your sex life starts to dwindle, almost to the point where it becomes non-existent, and you both are still sleeping in the same bed at night, she may be cheating. Remember, women love sex too. If she not getting it from you, she's getting it from someone else, unless she has taken a vow of celibacy, without bothering to tell you about it.

13. Here is a doozy. Be careful of your lady's male friends. Some women who had male friends before they met you may not want to stop being friends with those guys. If you and she start having problems, she may confide in her friends. You know how most women love to talk and spill their guts about what they are going through. That can be a bad thing, because what man doesn't want to play hero for a woman in

distress? Her friend may start to do things or say things to make her happy, and that may make her vulnerable; willing to reward him with some sex, especially if the problems between you and her persist. Women can have friends of the opposite sex and have a man she's dating or married to, but there has to be some boundaries in place. Lots of cheating happens because of a "friend" who was available in a time of need. Pay attention to those "friends" fellas. They can be sneaky; just waiting for you to slip up.

14. This is a good one: If your lady has a habit of starting petty arguments with you, and leaving the home to "cool off", pay attention to her moves. This could be a ploy for her to go and see another man. Women can be really sneaky, fellas.

15. Check this one out: If she considers you a weak man and someone who doesn't stand up for yourself or her, when it counts, she

may undoubtedly cheat on you at some point. Women love a man with a backbone and they love a man who displays strength, even with her when she gets out of line at times. Weakness in a man is a huge turnoff to women.

16. Another good one: If you're the type of man who works a lot and she complains about your workload, pay attention to her moves. If you like to work and provide for who you have, but she thinks you work too much, to the point where she starts to feel 'lonely', she may be beginning to see another man on the side. This type of stuff does happen, fellas. Stay alert. Hard to believe, but some women don't appreciate a hard-working man.

17. Here is a powerful point to think about, fellas. If you ever find yourself sick, dealing with some serious health issues, and your lover or spouse is not there helping you and comforting you, this is a huge sign that they

may be cheating. Most people can't deal with illnesses, and as crazy as it sounds, they may feel "inconvenienced" by your sickness. They may become distant and somewhat insensitive to your unfortunate situation. If you find this happening to you, watch how your partner is handling all of this. They may feel justified by cheating on you, because you are sick and they are not. You can't move around and they can. Not one of us can help becoming sick sometimes, and it's not right that the person who says they love you feels that it is bad that you can't move around and have fun with them. This happens ALL of the time. So, stay alert and be aware.

18. If you are dating or married to a woman who is a teacher of young, adolescent teens, keep an eye on her! The rise of older women sleeping with and messing around with teen boys, and teen girls (hey, it's real out here), is growing year by year. Of course, this is crazy and often criminal, in

the eyes of the law, but a lot of these women have husbands and children. Your wife/girlfriend is not exempt from either seducing a young person, or being seduced by a young person. It's true!

19. If you are living with a woman and she is carrying most of the financial load in that household, deep down she may not respect you as a man and she may at some point start cheating on you with someone with some money! Women love a responsible man: responsible men handle their business.

20. Another one and a real doozy: If your wife/girlfriend has a "special" female friend that she is always hanging around, you may want to ask your lady if her "friend" is heterosexual. If by chance, her friend doesn't like men, but likes women, pay close attention to how they behave around each other. Her "friend" may be trying to convert your lady into a part-time "coochie-

eater". This can spell big trouble for your union. I'm not being facetious here, fellas. This has happened and is happening all over the world today.

21. Here is one to really think about fellas: Be careful if you find yourself with a "needy" woman. If she is always calling you, texting you, and wanting to be all under you when you and she are together, this is not normal behavior. This woman may have some underlining issues, where she may not be fully trusting with her man. If you call her out on her needy ways, be careful, because this may prompt her to get with another man who will accommodate her need to be needy. Absence and time apart make the heart grow fonder.

22. Okay, fellas, here is one for the ages: If you are currently with a woman that you got with by cheating, meaning that she was already with another man when you and she got together, just know that how you

got her is how you will probably lose her. In other words, if she cheated WITH you, she will probably end up cheating ON you. What goes around, comes back around, just so you know.

23. Watch out for the exes. If your wife or girlfriend has an ex-lover that she is still cool with and she occasionally keeps in touch with this person, be on the alert. The flame that they had for each other may not be fully extinguished and she could easily rekindle her flame for this guy. How many women have cheated on their current husband or boyfriend with an ex-lover? Too many to count, believe me. Stay alert. Watch for the signs. Cheating happens all the time. Oftentimes, the person cheating is doing so with an ex-lover.

24. Here is another powerful one that many of us men don't think about: If you have a male friend who tells you that he believes your woman may be cheating on you,

always check with your lady first before taking your friend's word for it. I put this one in here because there have been people who have secretly wanted to be with their friend's lover, and in order to make that happen, they would be sneaky and low-down enough to plant seeds of doubt in their friend's mind about the person that they are with. You good friend can turn out to be your worst enemy, especially when a good-looking woman is involved, so be careful and stay alert. Sadly, it's like that sometimes.

25. Last one fellas. Most women have had their fathers in their lives. If he was the type of man that was a great man, handled his business well and was responsible for his family, those women will sometimes compare any man they date to their fathers. If your lady complains, even in the least bit, about how you handle yourself and if she has a habit of comparing you to how her father was, you need to pay

attention to this. Women desire to be with a man who matches up with the type of man their fathers were, and if you are not matching up to those standards, she may be enticed to cheat on you with a man who does match up. Pay close attention to your lady in this important regard.

These are some things you as men can take and run with as you date and get married. Sadly, we live in a world where people do things that don't make sense most of the times to you, but it makes them happy.

These signs that I have listed here are things that you can watch out for if, and only if, you suspect that things are going somewhat sideways in your relationship/marriage. Above all, I implore you to maintain happiness and harmony with the one you love, but at the same time, be vigilant, whenever and however the situation warrants it.

Chapter 10
Your Words Can Control Your Relationship

This particular chapter is one that I truly hope will touch the heart of the reader, especially if you don't understand how powerful your words are. Now, you may ask yourself "what do my words have to do with my relationship?" The answer to that is this: Everything! Your words have everything to do with the success or failure of who you're with.

I'm going to mainly approach my point from how negative words can affect what you have. For example, remember how I said in the beginning of this book that I was a frequent watcher of the TV show "Cheaters"? Well, some of that has given me the ammunition to write this book. There was one particular episode where the woman believed her live-in boyfriend was seeing another woman. She employed the Cheaters crew to follow him around and gather proof of her suspicions, and sure enough, he was cheating with another woman.

Well, if you're familiar with the format of that show, you already know what happened. She and the camera crew confronted him with the other woman, and all hell broke loose. Fast forward to the ending segment: the boyfriend said something that I thought was poignant and very interesting. He said this about his now ex-girlfriend: *"She was the love of my life, but she was always accusing me of cheating on her. It went on and on, and I finally thought that since she kept on verbally accusing me of cheating, I might as well go out and start cheating"*.

Now, do you see what happened here? He said that she kept on "verbally" accusing him of cheating. Whether she had proof or not that he was actually cheating on her, she was unknowingly using her own words to push her man into the arms of another woman. Now, like I said in the first chapter, there is never an excuse to cheat, and her boyfriend was wrong to cheat on his live-in girlfriend. But, without knowing what she was doing, she partially contributed to the demise of her relationship.

Her accusatory words worked against her, because the man felt somehow empowered to cheat on her, even though that is not what she wanted, obviously. By her continuing to say things like "you must be seeing someone else", or "I think you're cheating on me" or "you better not be seeing another woman", she was hurting her relationship with her words. I'm not certain if there was a past hurt that this woman suffered from and never got over; one that she eventually brought into her new relationship with this man. But, whatever the case was, with her constant verbal accusations of cheating, she subconsciously spoke death to her relationship with this man. In other words, what she was verbally accusing him of came true.

What is even sadder than her catching her man with another woman is the fact that she may never realize what she did by verbally accusing him of cheating all of the time like she had done. Believe it or not, this is a powerful thing. Unless you have concrete proof that your lover is cheating on you, you never want to verbally accuse them of cheating on you, constantly, because if you do, this could be your fate.

I have read other stories of people who dealt with the same thing. Guys cheating on their ladies, only to come back and say "she was always accusing me. I don't know why I cheated, but she was accusing me when I wasn't. What was I supposed to do"? Or the ladies being accused by a paranoid husband/boyfriend, only to finally cheat on him and not have a viable explanation other than to say "well, he always thought I was seeing someone else, and then he started accusing me of doing it. So, I figured why not".

I suppose that it's in some people's nature to be defensive when they suspect that their lover may be doing them wrong, but I'll say it again. If you suspect that your lover is cheating, but you don't have solid proof of it, watch your words regarding what you suspect. You could very well speak death to your marriage/relationship by always verbally accusing them of cheating.

Now, what you could try doing is speaking positive over your relationship. You could say things to your lover like "no one is going to treat you better than I treat you", or "you'll miss my loving if we ever broke up", or "I'm the best thing that's ever happened to you". Saying things like this to your lover will encourage confidence and it will let them know what a mistake they will make if they ever thought of cheating on you. Words do matter!

It also helps to have absolute trust in what you have, because at the end of the day, you can't control someone's actions. If they really wanted to cheat, they could. Therefore, what you don't want to do is subconsciously give them ammunition to cheat.

Now, ask yourself this. Have you ever been in a relationship, or were married at one point, and you were accusing your spouse/lover of cheating? Did your union end up ending due to cheating? Were you ever paranoid to the point where if they were not in your presence, you thought they were out with another person? Were you yourself ever in a situation where you were constantly accused of cheating, you weren't cheating then but did eventually ended up cheating? Do you see where I'm going here?

Accusing someone of cheating or being accused of cheating yourself will no doubt lead to someone "actually" cheating at some point, because of the power of words. It's somewhat hard to explain why this is, but just know that it does happen. Think of it like this: if you wake up one morning and you tell yourself that you're going to have a bad day, then there is a wonderful chance that your prediction will come true and your day will turn out the way you said it would: BAD.

The spoken word is a powerful thing, and too many people unknowingly use their words in a destructive way, especially where their relationships are concerned. The premise of this book is to help people be aware of things in case they suspect that cheating is going with the person that they're with. This book was also written as a tool to help people prevent relationship heartache as well. This chapter is a prime example of that.

If you want your union to be a vibrant and successful one, then you must understand how your words can help you, or hurt you, whichever you decide. Now, after reading this chapter, ask yourself this question: <u>How will I proceed with my spouse/lover in how I talk to them</u>? If you think that they may be cheating, but don't have proof, only speculation, be careful that you don't go accusing them of cheating. Stay alert, proceed with caution and choose your words carefully.

Chapter 11
Signs for the Ladies
(What to Watch Out For)

Well ladies, I have saved the best for last here. You don't like it when the man in your life strays, and that is completely understandable. But, so many do stray and for many men, they do it out of boredom or for reasons that sometimes can't be explained. What I want to do here is give you ladies some signs to look for if you suspect that husband/boyfriend of yours is stepping out on you with another woman. I can speak as a man and I know how men think for the most part, when they want to be sneaky and conniving.

Now, before I start with this, I just want to say that if you ever think that there is some funny business going on with your man, keep your eyes open and have some concrete proof. If you don't do that, and you accuse him of cheating, he may try to turn it around and say that you're doing the very thing you're accusing him of doing. Have your ducks in a row before you go to making accusations. I had to add that in here, just like I did for the fellas. With that being said, here are some signs:

1. If you are dating a man whom after some time has passed, he doesn't seem inclined to invite you to his home, this could mean one of two things: 1) he could want to avoid the temptation of having sex with you if you do come over, or, 2) he could be already living with a woman, namely his wife/girlfriend and he is cheating on her with YOU. Some of these dudes out here are grimy and heartless, just being honest.

2. If you meet a man, started dating him and after perhaps six months, you decide to have sex with him, make sure that he wears a condom. If he refuses and then tries to convince you to let him "hit it raw", watch out! Just know that you are more than likely NOT the only woman he's sleeping with. You are probably part of his stable of women, and chances are that this clown is packing an STD. You don't want to play with your health, right? Be smart and stay alert.

3. Ladies, if your man begins to make snide remarks about your weight, first off he's being a jerk. Also, if he starts comparing you to other "sexy" women and feels that you should look like some other woman, this may be a sign that he's looking in another direction for satisfaction and he may be cheating on you. Your man should be happy with you, regardless of what you look like or how much you weigh. Remember this phrase: "Beautiful body, Gorgeous mind".

4. If your husband/boyfriend tends to have a bunch of "female friends", be careful of this. Chances are he's already slept with a few of them and it wouldn't take much for his to start back up sleeping with them, despite having you in his life. Some men just loving having women around them.

5. Ladies, watch how a man treats his mother. If he treats her with love and respect, then chances are he'll do right by you. But, if he's disrespectful to the person who birthed him

into the world, then you definitely don't stand a chance. He's bound to dog out any woman in his life. Facts!!!

6. If the man in your life has a habit of lying to you, even about perceived small things, this is someone you definitely don't need in your life. Liars are annoying as hell, and eventually you won't be able to believe anything they say. There are men out here who are willing to be truthful to you, always. Find one of those men and don't drive yourself crazy by being with a liar. Liars are synonymous with cheaters; like a hand in glove.

7. Be careful of a man who watches a lot of porn. Pornography has the power to corrupt the mind and it paints unrealistic expectations of sex for people. If he wants you to perform sexually like the porn stars he watches and you refuse to do so, he may end up cheating on you to have his desires met. Men like this don't realize that those

women are paid to act out those sexually explicit scenes.

8. Ladies, no matter how much he begs you or if he offers to buy you something nice, you must never agree to do a threesome with your husband/boyfriend and another woman. If you do, just one time, you will be opening "Pandora's Box" in your relationship, and that box may never close. This may prompt him to want to experiment without you in the mix, only for him to twist it, flip it and blame you for him stepping out on you. If you can't be enough woman for him sexually, then he doesn't need to be with you. Tell him to "kick rocks".

9. Here's a really good one: If your man exhibits any type of tendencies whereby he maybe into men, don't ignore this! Some men out here are very much into men, but they are in heavy denial about this, so they won't admit their truth to themselves, and

certainly not to you. They believe that they still want to be with a woman, but they may start hanging out with men, on the low; having sex with other men and bringing possible STD's home to you. This is so real that's it is not funny. Make sure you pay attention when you have an inkling of funny business going on with your man. So many women's lives are ruined today because of a "Down Low" man that was in denial about his sexuality.

10. If your husband/boyfriend has a habit of looking at other women while you and he are out in public together, if it bothers you, let him know about it right away. If it persists even after you told him to knock it off, rethink what you have with this guy. He may have it in him to do more than just look, especially when you're not around him. A man has to have self-control.

11. If you're dating or married to a professional athlete, understand that these guys have

"coochie and booty" thrown at them all of the time. The best thing that can be done is for you both to establish an understanding that no matter how much money he's paid or how popular he is, you will NOT put up with a "wayward penis". So what if he has money, what woman knowingly and willingly wants to be with a philandering man?

12. Here is one that will make you think: If you are a wealthy woman, and you're with a man that doesn't have the money that you have, pay close attention to his character. Please understand that he could still cheat on you, even if you are spending mad loot on him, buying him nice, expensive items. In other words, never try to buy a man's love, affection and companionship. You can still be betrayed in your generosity to a man. Real talk.

13. Ladies, if you husband/boyfriend loves, and I mean loves frequenting strip clubs and

titty bars, this could be a problem down the road with you and him. There are many tantalizing women working in those places and the temptation to "sample" the eye candy might be too much for him to resist. Those places breed a spirit of lust and fantasies, and that can be unhealthy for a marriage/relationship. Stay alert ladies.

14. This is a huge one ladies: If you are married to or dating a preacher/minister, you have to watch how they interact with other women. Some of these so called "men of the cloth" are the biggest liars, pimps, players, frauds, and whoremongers on the planet. For some reason women tend to throw themselves at pastors and ministers by the dozen. Ladies, your man could be preaching behind the pulpit on Sunday morning, and sexing other women on Sunday night. This is the honest to God truth! Watch that preacher man of yours, because they slip and fall just like the rest of us.

15. I said this to the fellas, and I'm saying it to you as well. If you or your man is military, make certain that there is an understanding between you both about fidelity and what is to be expected. You may feel the urge to get your "swerve on" with another man, if your main man is thousands of miles away, and vice versa for your man. One of his female military counterparts can play "wifey" to him and break him off some loving without you knowing. If you can't stand being away from your man for long periods of time, you may want to reconsider being with that man. Just being honest.

16. Watch out for the exes. If your husband or boyfriend has an ex-lover that he is still cool with and he occasionally keeps in touch with this person, be on the alert. The flame that they had for each other may not be fully extinguished. He could easily rekindle his flame for this woman. How many men have cheated on their current wife or

girlfriend with an ex-lover? Too many to count, believe me. Stay alert. Watch for the signs. Cheating happens all the time. Oftentimes, the person cheating is doing so with an ex-lover.

17. This is one that almost ALL women can relate to: Ladies, any man who is honest with you, faithful to you, truthful with you, and respectful of you will have NO issue with you seeing his phone. Yes, his cell phone! How many men out here have text messages, pictures, and other incriminating stuff from other women on their phones and they are scared that their wives/girlfriends would discover their madness? If he's not cheating on you, he should have nothing to hide on his phone, right? Of course, we're all entitled to our privacy, but a guilty conscious will always have something to hide. If he is hesitant to let you see his phone, that's a red flag!!

18. Be careful when dating a tattoo artist, photographer, masseuse, or a politician, ladies. Men with these professions meet a lot of women and statistics show that the divorce rate for people in these fields is somewhat high. Business can turn into pleasure quickly in these categories. Set some boundaries with your man if he happens to have one of the above occupations. Stay alert.

19. Ladies, pay close attention to this one: If you ever find yourself with a man who feels like you have to "need" him in order to validate you and him being together, this is a huge sign of bad things to come. This type of "man" does indeed possess the capacity to cheat on you, if you don't give him some sick sense of assurance that the woman he is with has to "need" him. Any man who is built like this will only be happy with "needy" women; not strong and solid women, those who are the total opposite of a "needy" woman. Avoid any man like the

one described here. This type of "man" will eventually cheat on you, only to satisfy his ego, as if to say that he's doing you a favor by being with you. Real talk ladies.

20. Here is a powerful point to think about ladies. If you ever find yourself sick and dealing with some serious health issues, and your lover or spouse is not there helping you and comforting you, this is a huge sign that they may be cheating. Most people can't deal with illnesses. As crazy as it sounds, they may feel "inconvenienced" by your sickness. They may become distant and somewhat insensitive to your unfortunate situation. If you find this happening to you, watch how your partner is handling all of this. They may feel justified by cheating on you, because you are sick and they are not. You can't move around and they can. Not one of us can help becoming sick sometimes, and it's not right that the person who says they love you feels that it is bad that you can't move

around and have fun with them. This happens ALL of the time so stay alert and be aware.

21. Ladies, I hate to say this one, but I have to speak the truth... You have to watch your female relatives around your man. If you have a sister or cousin who may try to flirt with your husband/boyfriend, even innocently, check them immediately. That man may come to believe that he can have you and that female relative of yours. Also, if you have a female roommate that you are living with, and you have a boyfriend that comes by frequently, keep your eyes open! You would be surprised at how your friend/female roommate would cheat with your man, and feel nothing about it. Families and relationships have been torn apart and shattered by all of these scenarios, real talk. Stay alert always in this regard.

22. Ladies, if your husband/boyfriend is an entertainer, be sure to watch out for his moves, as best as you can. There is a real famous singer that shall remain nameless, and her equally famous husband cheated on her. Now, being as pretty as she is, you would think that there is no way she would be cheated on, right? Well, that just goes to show you that you can be very attractive and famous, but if a man wants to cheat, he's going to cheat, and his fame may make it easier. Stay alert and watch out for groupies. They don't respect your union, at all.

23. Here we go ladies: If your man starts to fall off from having sex with you or wanting to have sex with you, and you know that this man loves and needs sex, this man is getting sex, just not from you!! Ask him straight up who he's getting his sexual gratification from, and don't take any of his lies. Men need sex, because they need that semen release.

24. Ladies, this is one that many of you have fallen victim to: Don't be so quick to tell your female friends about how great of a lover your man is. There are not that many eligible men out here, and if you have what many would consider a good catch, and you like to express what a great lover he is, chances are that they don't want a man like your man, they may want YOUR MAN! That so-called good friend of yours may be bold enough to get at your man behind your back, letting him know that if you ever mess up, he can come running to her. This does happen ladies, and it has happened to many women. Keep your lips zipped and don't talk about your man to other women, not even your friends, because they can plot to be with your man. Who's to say that your man won't take the bait? This sounds crazy, but it's the truth!

25. I told the fellas this, and now I'm telling you.... If the man that you are currently with was someone that already had a woman

when you and he got together, and you are now his main lady, look out! If he cheated WITH you, there is a great chance that he will end up cheating ON you. You reap what you sow in this life. Never forget that!

26. Here is a powerful one for you ladies to think about: If you and your man love to travel and see different places, either for business or pleasure, you have to maintain this for the happiness and success of your union. If you find that your man has begun to not want you going with him on trips, this may be a huge sign of trouble. What man does not want his lady accompanying him on a trip away from home, unless you just can't go with him? Not saying that you both need to be joined at the hip, but if he starts subtly taking trips without you with him, he may just be going to see another woman. This does happen ladies, so stay alert and pay attention. If he's cheating on you, it doesn't have to be with women who live in the same city, state or country.

27. Last one ladies. If you are a virgin and you have made a choice to stay a virgin until your wedding night, just know that the men you date will have to decide to respect your decision. However, try not to be surprised if any man you date gets some "coochie" from other women, all while trying to be the man who waits to marry you. If he's getting sex before he "supposedly" marries you, don't you think he'll get some sex from other women after he marries you? Think about what I'm saying here and stick to your guns.

Well, I did what I could in explaining to you wonderful ladies some of the things men tend to do when they may be out cheating or on the cusp of seeing another woman. Like I said, I was not pulling any punches nor taking any prisoners in this book. My hope with this book is to open many peoples' eyes as to some intricate things that happen when cheating takes place.

There may be other signs that I didn't list here, but hopefully you get the gist of what I did put forth. Be aware of things that people go through.

At the end of the day, maintain love, peace and harmony in your marriage/relationship, but, be aware of the signs of possible misgivings. You owe it to yourself not to be played by the one you love, although, at times, everyone plays the fool.

Chapter 12
A Little Something for the College Students

I had to add a chapter in this thought-provoking book for any and all of my college kids. I understand that many of you find love in a place of higher learning. This is completely understandable. But, there are some things that you all, young men and young women, have to understand when dating in college. I'm going to be as real as I can with you, so please take in what I have written herein.

First thing is, you have to know that youth will play a huge role in potential "stupidity" either on your side or the person you choose to be with. What I mean by that is you both are young and still trying to find yourselves, in addition to acquiring an education. You may make some unwise choices / decisions in your young life, and for the most part, this is normal. I'll break down some things for the ladies first, and then the fellas.

For the Ladies

Ok ladies, here is where I turn you all onto some really important game when dating these young men on these college campuses. Please know that many of them are not going to be mature enough to want to handle being with one young lady. Why? Because wherein that young man might see something wonderful in you, he may see a ton of things he likes, or thinks he likes in other women. What is to stop him from seeing you and a bunch of other young women on the same campus, at the same time? That is the question you have to ask yourself. In addition, you have to ask, "Is this what I want?" The chances of this happening are very high.

A young man in his late teens or early 20's doesn't really know what he wants in a woman, but he does know that he wants a woman with big breasts, a big butt, a pretty face, and to see if she's willing to "give up the coochie" at any given moment. Most young, male college students want those things in a woman.

And here is the interesting thing ladies: you could be one of the prettiest girls on the entire campus, and you could be giving him what he wants sexually (not that you should be), and he will STILL cheat on you with other women, mostly because he's stupid and has no self-control. Why do you think that these young men do that? I'll tell you why, because for a lot of them, it's like being a kid in a candy store.

These young men see so many pretty young women on campus, and for the most part, monogamy is not a high priority for them. Another thing that you have to watch out for is fraternities. A lot of these fraternities are full of men who do nothing but party, step, and run women! Don't be surprised ladies if you ever date a Frat, and you catch him cheating on you with a dozen other women.

These dudes are popular on campus. They have young women throwing themselves at guys all the time. All I'm saying ladies is that you have your whole lives ahead of you. You don't have to let some young knucklehead break your heart because you think you're in love, only to realize that he doesn't feel the same about you that you feel about him.

I want to encourage you all that your primary focus should be on your studies, getting phenomenal grades and eventually, getting that college degree. The dudes will be there after you accomplish your reason for being in college. What you don't want to have happen is for some young idiot to get you caught up, tripped up, and knocked up with his baby, only for him to possibly abandon you and act as if your getting pregnant was your own fault. Subsequently, he leaves you for some other young woman, and now you're sad, heartbroken and angry in the process.

This does happen ladies, so take heed. Lots of cheating happens on college campuses; with most young men who are only trying to get as much sex as they can from whoever is giving it up. Live your lives and date who you please, but just know that if you see some "signs" of potential cheating and two-timing from the young men, there is good chance that it's happening. Please allow me to add this as well…. If you are sexually active, be certain that you are using protection each and every time you have sex. No exceptions!

If he tries to convince you to let him "hit it raw", DON'T DO IT! Make him wear a condom every time and make certain that he doesn't take it off during sex. Many of these young men are ruthless and they don't really care about getting you pregnant and leaving you to hold the bag all by yourself. These young men will come and go, but you have to be focused on what's really important: getting that degree!

I want to add this last point ladies…. If you are dating a young man and you're attending a college or university that is in a city different than the city that your boyfriend lives in, be absolutely sure that you and he understand that you may not be able to see each other all of the time. Please note that the young man you're dating may be inclined to see a woman that's closer to him than you are.

Understand this: he's young and he may want to 'sow some wild oats', especially if you and he are in a long-distance relationship where he doesn't see you all of the time. He may not have the patience to date a young woman who's away at college in another city. While he may not be mature enough to tell you this, he may opt to start cheating instead. Acts of this nature tend to be very common, so always stay alert and focused.

For the Fellas

Okay, young men, I have told the young ladies about how many of you get down while in college. Now I want to tell you all some things as well about the young ladies you'll encounter. More than likely, the women will outnumber you all 3 to 1, which is to be expected. I know that many of you will love that, because you will have so many young women to choose from. I want to try to encourage you to not become college playboys. For the most part, you are there to learn and to obtain a college education, not to pull women and to become "college Casanovas".

Now that I've gotten that out of the way, understand this as well. Some of the young ladies you attend school with won't be the helpless 'dummies' that men tend to think they are. Many of them will be players and flirts, just like some men tend to be. Some of these young ladies will have a mindset to make a man finance her college lifestyle. What I mean is that you can meet a girl, start to court her and before you know it, you and she are a couple.

But, if she has a "sack chaser" mentality, meaning she wants a man with big money, and you don't fit that description, she may have you and one or several other dudes in her life at the same time. Remember, just like many of you can be knuckleheads, some of the young women may possess the same characteristics as well. This is something that you may not be aware of. Most women love a man with intellect. Yes, they love a man who is a thinker and is prone to use his brain. So, if you're a jock on campus, don't make the mistake of thinking that this is all it takes to get a woman. That young lady you have been dating can cheat on you with a "nerd", but that nerd is smart and intelligent, making him attractive to your woman. Also, you have to watch out for women who love to flirt with other men, even if they say that there is nothing to their flirting.

A lot of young women can be swayed by other men who will promise them the world, something you might not be up on doing. Be leery of the young ladies who may have a reputation of being college flirts and floozies. I'm not trying to dump on the ladies, just simply stating facts. Some of these young women tend to gravitate towards the so called "bad boys" on campus, and if you don't consider yourself a bad boy, leave women like this completely alone, because they could end up hurting you.

Also, don't let a woman use you just to make another man jealous. Some people don't handle jealously well, and you could end up in the middle of some drama that might not end well for you. I'm just saying.

Here is one very important point I want to make: If you ever have a situation where a young woman is accusing you of possibly being the father of her unborn child, and you know you slept with her with no protection, there is a chance that you may be the father, but here is what you do. Don't let her convince you to sign ANYTHING until after the baby is born, and then you demand a DNA test to determine if you really are the father or not.

One of the worst things that can happen to a young man, one with his whole life ahead of him is to sign a birth certificate of a baby that he determines is NOT biologically his, but due to either the state in which the baby was born or the state in which you reside, you could be legally on the hook for the support that child. This has happened to many unsuspecting naïve young men who weren't smart enough to think before they acted.

I will conclude on this matter, for now. But, hopefully all of you young men and women in college will take heed to what I've written here in this thought-provoking book about cheating. It's my hope that you will be smart in your young lives and not allow careless mistakes to hinder your educational endeavors. Peep game, young people. Be well on your life's journey.

Chapter 13
The Wrap-Up

So, in conclusion of writing this book, I hope that what I've done was shown you, the reader, that cheating is wrong overall, but that it does happen and has been happening for years and years. Relationships take work, plenty of work, nonstop work, and when a couple doesn't put in the work needed to be successful and stay committed to each other, monotony seeps in and one person in the union may look outside for gratification, without wanting to leave the current union.

I can say without reservation, that the cheater is being selfish: bottom line. Now, is it a surprise that when a marriage/relationship gets to a point of boredom, the person feeling bored and unfulfilled may want to be with another person? No, it's not a surprise, but instead of wanting to be with someone else, what would be the logical thing to do is to communicate your feelings with your lover; let them know that the union is currently not fulfilling. Attempt to fix it and keep things rolling.

But, in all of the signs that I listed for the men and women here in this book to watch out for, people are not quick on the logical side of things, because logic for most people requires work. So, let's be real; people who cheat on their lovers are lazy. Yes, a person who is cheating is attempting to juggle what they have in their lover, while seeing someone else at the same time in secret. This can be taxing, but it's lazy because you're spreading yourself between multiple people…you have to start lying to maintain what you think is a good set up.

But, the reality is, is that most people who cheat eventually get exposed, because they can only carry on with so many lies for so long, and at some point, the person that they are cheating with may not want to be a secret for too long. They'll figure since you're spending time with them, the time that you could be spending with your lover, you must not be happy and they'll wonder why not just break things off with your lover and be with them full time. That is where things can get really hazy.

Remember the movie *Fatal Attraction*? Yes, that crazy movie. Glenn Close's character didn't want to continue being the mistress to Michael Douglas' character. It was fine in the beginning when he was coming over and having sex with her behind his wife's back, but it got to a point where she wanted more from him. She wanted to be the new main lady in his life. In other words, he could only continue to have his cake in being with his wife and eating it too, by sleeping with his mistress, for only so long.

At some point, it all blew up in his face, because his wife found out about his affair, and she was NONE too happy about it. This is how it always turns out for someone who cheats on their spouse/lover. Your whole deceptive behavior is exposed. In most cases, you could end up losing not only your spouse/lover, but your new conquest as well, depending on the type of person they are.

In all honesty, it's really not worth it to cheat and lie, but I realize that people are going to do what they want to do. At the end of the day, no one can stop an adult, male or female, from doing what they want to do. Hopefully, what I have presented in this book are some things that you can look for if you think that the person you've been with for a while is cheating on you.

Think of this book as somewhat of an educational piece that you can have for as long as you live and love. The person you meet, fall in love with and grow with can change on you, unfortunately for the worst, sometimes. It's important for you not to be a fool for love. Stay on point... be aware of some of the underhanded deeds people do to the ones they say they love. Love can be a battle field. This book can be your weapon to protect yourself from undue heartache. Peace be unto you.

Bonus Chapter:
You Find Out That They Have Indeed Cheated; Now What?

Well, you have read some of the signs that I believe people engage in when they may be cheating with another person. Now, let's take it a step further. What happens when you find out that the person that you're married to or having been dating for some time has been indeed cheating on you with another person? What do you do? Well, while no one can tell you what to do exactly, I'll do my best to give some heartfelt advice.

Of course, when one finds out that they have been betrayed by their lover, all types of thoughts rush through their minds. Hurt, anger, confusion, shock, more anger, and a lack of understanding as to why this has happened to them. These feelings are all understandable, even predictable. But, here is the hard truth. When you find out that cheating has happened, what you shouldn't do is stay there in those feelings and wallow in them, in a state of disbelief.

Yes, you are going to hurt and probably hurt for a long time, but the question you have to ask yourself is how long will you allow this hurt to stay in your being. Only you can answer that for yourself, but here is some reality to consider when deciding what to do in moving forward in your life. The person who cheated on you, you can either forgive them, attempt to repair your fractured union, in an attempt to keep it together. You can choose not to forgive them, divorce or break up. But, what you don't want to do is torture yourself.

Now what do I mean when I say torture yourself? What I mean is you don't want to stay with that person out of some obligation, but then choose to stay mad and pissed off whenever you think about what they did to you by cheating. You're both living in the same house, but there is no communication, no togetherness, no sex, no nothing.

For some reason, you want to stay mad at that person, but you don't want to break up or leave them, and you don't want them to leave you. That is torture, because your mind is consumed with their betrayal. For whatever the reason may be, you remain a part of the union with them. Here's the thing. If you are going to stay with them after they have done this thing, then you're going to have to forgive them and start fresh. Because, if you don't, you'll never have that inner peace that we all deserve to have in this brief life. Not only that, but the trust has to be rebuilt between the both of you. Otherwise, if you can't trust someone, you shouldn't be with them.

This is it in a nutshell, and it doesn't matter if you're young and just starting out in love or older and have seen some things. Sometimes, cheating happens and while it's unfortunate, how you choose to bounce back is what's important. Forgive, rebuild and stay or break it off and move on completely, no gray area in this. The choice is yours. Choose wisely.

Extra Bonus Chapter:
"Age Ain't Nothing But A Number"...,
Or So They Say

Just when I thought I was done with writing this book, so much pertinent information come rushing in my head that I needed to get into this book for many to be aware of. I listed a bunch of signs that people need to be aware of when they suspect that the person they are with may be cheating on them. In addition to what I have written in the prior pages, I have to mention that a significant age gap can somewhat guarantee that a person will cheat.

I'll attempt to explain what I mean by this. People like to say that when it comes to age, it's nothing but a number. While I can agree with that to a certain extent, it does at some point play into a relationship. For example, you can have a 41-year-old man that is dating a 25-year-old woman. In the beginning, they meet each other, and exchange phone numbers.

Then, they begin to talk over the phone, building rapport with one another: getting to know each other. Then, they start meeting up, going out on dates and spending time with each other. All of a sudden, they become a couple. Now, realize that there is a 16-year age difference between the two of them, meaning that he was sixteen when she was born. You have a generational gap here. While she was a baby, this guy was preparing to graduate high school. While she was learning how to walk, talk and potty-train, he was probably in college, living life.

Fast forward some years. Now, she's getting ready to enter adulthood and this guy has lived life some. They meet through some chance encounter and they are a couple. While they try and make it work as a couple, despite their age difference, after some time together, the age difference begins to become a problem.

The older boyfriend perhaps can't really relate to the type of music that the younger girlfriend likes to listen to, or the younger girlfriend perhaps doesn't like that the older boyfriend is a home body and she likes to go out and party with her friends. Here is the thing. If I had to take a guess as to who would probably cheat in this instance, I would say that it would probably be the girlfriend. Why do I say this? Because she is younger and probably not very mature as how to handle having an older person as a lover.

Sure, she loves her man, but with him being older than she, her footloose and fancy-free attitude would probably give her cause to cheat. There is a good chance she would cheat with a man around her own age. Now, would she break up with her older boyfriend and start seeing another man altogether? Probably not, because her older boyfriend would no doubt be the type of man who is spending money on her, doing things for her that she would not want to stop.

She would continue to be with her older boyfriend, all while seeing other men around her own age. In the beginning, the age difference was not a problem, because they were trying something new and fresh, with her dating an older and somewhat established man, and him dating a younger and sexy woman; probably eye candy. But after some time had passed, the things that weren't age-related issues at first, had started to become issues.

So, in essence, age was NOT just a number. This is what people need to understand when they desire to be with someone who is somewhat far from their age. As hard as you two may try, you can't completely overlook the age difference. You have to factor in the life difference you have with that person.

Another example. If an older woman desires to date a younger man who's into older women, that may work out for a while, but at some point, that younger man may start to desire women his own age. What is to stop him from seeing women around his age, while continuing to see the "cougars" he wants to be with? Nothing. So understand that just because you and the person you're seeing has an age gap between you can be fine and wonderful, you both are going to have to work hard to maintain the love, respect and trust needed to keep things going.

You both are going to have to love the same things, and be willing to sacrifice certain things to stay together. The generational gap can be a problem down the road. Truthfully, it almost always is when it comes to being with someone older or younger than you. In addition, for the older women who has a penchant for younger me...please be careful, ladies. There are a lot of young men out here who have a thing for older women. (I must acknowledge that some of these women who are of a certain age are blessed not to look their age.) But, ladies, you have to watch out for what I call "game". Yes, many of these young cats tend to run "game" on older women, telling them things that they think they want to hear, doing things for them, all so that they can get money from them, sex from them and/or get them to pay their rent. I've seen this happen to many unsuspecting older women, thinking that they're "lucky" to have a young, strong, virile man. Only to find out that he's been playing her and using her for selfish reasons.

They find out that he was never really in love with them, he was only using them to get what he wanted, all while being with and sexing up other women, around their own age. This is one big reason why I wrote this book, to expose some of the ways of conniving people are out here running "game". Cheating is wrong and it shouldn't matter if there is an age difference. No one deserves to have their feelings and emotions played with, no matter how old they are.

Also, people should be mature enough and adult enough not to want to play with people's feelings and emotions, no matter how young or old they are. So, in summation of what I have just written in this extra bonus chapter, I would have to say that age really isn't just a number. We'd like to believe it is, but truthfully, it can be an eventual barrier when two people who differ significantly in age are together. At the end of the day, you have to respect the people who come into your life, young and old, because like that saying goes, "What goes around, comes back around". This rings true.

Discussion Questions

1. Are you a victim of infidelity/past cheating? If so, how did you handle it? Are you still with the person who cheated on you right now?
2. Do you think that "once a cheater, always a cheater" is true, or do you think that a person who cheats can reform and not ever cheat again?
3. If you discovered that a loved one or close friend of yours is being cheated on, would you inform them or let them discover it on their own?
4. Have you ever cheated on your lover? If so, did you confess your betrayal or did your lover find out?
5. Do you think that there is ever an excusable reason to cheat on someone?
6. Would you encourage people who were cheated on to stay and fix the union, or do you think they should cut their losses and break up/divorce?

7. Do you think it's possible to emotionally cheat and not physically cheat or are they one in the same?
8. What is your opinion on "taking breaks" in a relationship? Do you think that if a person does this and they go and sleep with someone else, is it cheating or not? What if they make a baby with the other person?
9. Do you think that "revenge cheating" is selfish or understandable?
10. If you ever had an opportunity to cheat without getting caught, would you do it?

www.ingramcontent.com/pod-product-compliance
Lightning Source LLC
Chambersburg PA
CBHW071406290426
44108CB00014B/1712